NATIONAL
GEOGRAPHIC

School Publishing

Food

James Nguyen

PICTURE CREDITS

Illustration by Roberto Fino (4–5).

Cover (left), 7 (below right), 15 (below right), Image Source; cover (right), 9 (above left & below right), 11, Lindsay Edwards Photography; 1, 2, 8, 9 (below left), 10, 12 (right), 13 (all), 14 (below left & below right), 16 (center left & below right), APL/Corbis; 6, 7 (above left), 15 (above right), 16 (above left), Photolibrary.com; 9 (above right), David R. Frazier Photolibrary, Inc./Alamy; 12 (left), Michelle Bridwell/PhotoEdit, Inc.; 14 (above left), Photodisc; 14 (above right), Amy Etra/PhotoEdit, Inc.; 15 (above left & below left), 16 (center right), Getty Images.

Produced through the worldwide resources of the National Geographic Society, John M. Fahey, Jr., President and Chief Executive Officer; Gilbert M. Grosvenor, Chairman of the Board; Nina D. Hoffman, Executive Vice President and President, Books and Education Publishing Group.

PREPARED BY NATIONAL GEOGRAPHIC SCHOOL PUBLISHING

Ericka Markman, Senior Vice President and President Children's Books and Education Publishing Group; Steve Mico, Senior Vice President and Publisher; Marianne Hiland, Editorial Director; Lynnette Brent, Executive Editor; Michael Murphy and Barbara Wood, Senior Editors; Bea Jackson, Design Director; David Dumo, Art Director; Margaret Sidlowsky, Illustrations Director; Matt Wascavage, Manager of Publishing Services; Sean Philpotts, Production Manager.

MANUFACTURING AND QUALITY MANAGEMENT

Christopher A. Liedel, Chief Financial Officer; Phillip L. Schlosser, Director; Clifton M. Brown III, Manager.

BOOK DEVELOPMENT

Ibis for Kids Australia Pty Limited.

Published by the National Geographic Society
1145 17th Street, N.W.
Washington, D.C. 20036-4688

ISBN-13: 978-0-792-26062-2
ISBN-10: 0-7922-6062-7

5 6 7 8 9 10   20 19 18 17
Printed in the United States of America

Contents

Fruit and Vegetables

Lettuce

Bananas

Watermelons

Oranges

Specials

Potatoes

Carrots

Onions

Corn

Tomatoes

Apples

Apple Juice

4

You can buy food at the supermarket. Where does the food come from?

Farms

Some food comes from farms.

Corn comes from farms.

Tomatoes come from farms.

Factories

Some food goes from farms to factories.

Corn can be made into tortillas.

Tomatoes can be made into salsa.

Supermarkets

Supermarkets sell food from farms and factories.

Shopping List
corn
tortillas
tomatoes
salsa

11

Let's Eat!

We use the food we buy to make meals.

bread

wheat plants

orange juice

orange tree

Which foods do you like to eat?
Where do these foods come from?

rice

rice plant

ketchup

tomato plant

corn

eat

factory

farm

food

supermarket

tomato

15

From Farm to Table

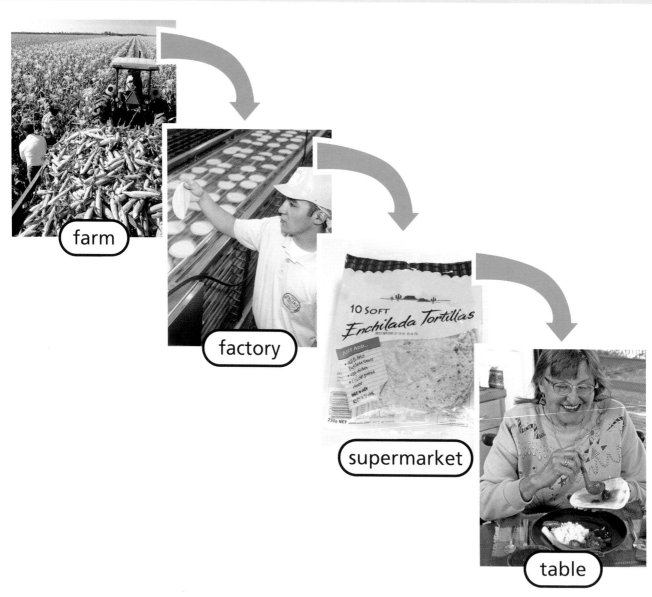

farm

factory

10 SOFT
Enchilada Tortillas

supermarket

table